cookies

Ivy Press

cookies

25 mouthwatering recipes

Susanna Tee

First published in 2008 by

Ivy Press
The Old Candlemakers
West Street, Lewes
East Sussex BN7 2NZ, UK
www.ivy-group.co.uk

Copyright © Ivy Press Limited 2008

ISBN-13: 978-1-905695-74-4
ISBN-10: 1-905695-74-8

Printed in China

10 9 8 7 6 5 4 3 2 1

Ivy Press
This book was conceived, designed
and produced by Ivy Press.

Creative Director Peter Bridgewater
Publisher Jason Hook
Editorial Director Caroline Earle
Art Director Clare Harris
Senior Editor Lorraine Turner
Senior Art Editor Sarah Howerd
Project Designer Joanna Clinch
Publishing Assistant Katie Ellis
Concept Design 'Ome Design
Photographer Jeremy Hopley
Food Stylist Susanna Tee

contents

introduction

A batch of freshly baked cookies is tempting to anyone. Making them yourself is particularly satisfying: handling the soft dough, the smell of baking wafting through the kitchen and, finally, the anticipation of that first, mouthwatering bite.

The recipes found in this book come from America, Australia, Great Britain and the rest of Europe. Whether you call them cookies or biscuits, these recipes are the very best from each country. The word 'biscuit' comes from the Latin words *bis coctum*, which means 'twice baked'. Biscuits were first made in ancient Egypt, although at that time they were discs of twice-cooked dough, which were given to sailors and soldiers because they kept so well. During the seventeenth century, sugar was added to sweeten them. At the same time, the number of domestic ovens increased, and cooks began to use a small quantity of cake mixture to test the temperature of their ovens before baking a cake, and so the biscuit became popular. It was the Dutch and German settlers who introduced them to North America, and the word 'cookie' comes from the Dutch word *koekje*, meaning 'little cake'.

Whatever you call them – and Australians use either term – make a batch of classic cookies today for the cookie jar or biscuit tin, to enjoy with friends over morning coffee; rustle up a tempting chocolate variety for a treat or special occasion; or, for some family bonding, get the children to help make their favourite cookies. It is an activity that they are sure to enjoy, and not just because they will be eating the results. Serving cookies to friends or giving them as gifts is all part of the fun of baking home-made cookies. Whatever the occasion, you will find your favourite recipe in this tempting collection.

the basics

Cookie baking is easy and requires very little special equipment apart from a few kitchen essentials. Simply follow these suggestions and useful tips to guarantee successful cookies every time.

Despite some oven manufacturers' instructions, you should preheat the oven for 10–15 minutes before you begin baking. Line baking trays with baking paper but, unless specified, do not grease because the dough will spread too much.

Use measuring scales and spoons because it is important that ingredients are measured accurately.

Butter or hard margarine is specified in the recipes: although butter is the best fat to use for flavour, margarine is less expensive and equally good. Choose a hard margarine that is labelled as intended for baking. Soft margarines are not suitable because they contain air and water. For blending, soften butter or margarine. Either leave it at room temperature for about 45 minutes, or take it out of the refrigerator, cut it into cubes, put it in a bowl and then microwave on High for 10 seconds.

If you do not have any self-raising flour, add 2½ teaspoons of baking powder to every 225 g/8 oz plain flour. Once the flour has been added, do not overbeat the dough or the cookies will be tough.

Useful tips

- Use a food processor only for rubbing fat into flour. When the eggs or liquid are added, blend quickly because overworked dough will make tough cookies.

- Place cookies on cold baking trays to prevent the dough from spreading excessively. Space them well apart to allow room for spreading. About 5 cm/2 in is usually about the correct space, unless they are very large.

- If baking more than one tray of cookies, change the baking trays round halfway through the cooking time. Don't position the lower tray too close to the one above because the cookies on it will not brown.

- Cool cookies on wire racks to prevent them from becoming soggy, and store them only when completely cold because they tend to stick together if still warm.

- Store soft and crisp cookies separately so that they don't all become soft.

a feast of cookies

cookie jar classics

shortbread rounds

walnut crunchies

butter fork cookies

cherry cookies

gingersnaps

almond macaroons

italian biscotti

lemon jumbles

orangines

chocolate temptations

rocky roads

dark chocolate cookies

chocolate chip cookies

chunky nut cookies

viennese fingers

caramel shortbread

no-cook chocolate bars

pinwheel cookies

children's favourites

peanut butter cookies

refrigerator cookies

apricot flapjacks

snowflake cookies

jumbo sultana cookies

gingerbread boys

iced cookie cutouts

coconut macaroons

shortbread rounds

Buttery, melt-in-the-mouth shortbread cookies are a true Scottish classic. If you have room for only one type of cookie in the cookie jar, these are definitely the ones to choose.

makes about 12

you will need

225 g/8 oz butter, softened

115 g/4 oz caster sugar, plus extra for dusting

225 g/8 oz plain white flour

115 g/4 oz ground rice or semolina

1 Put the butter and sugar in a large bowl and, using an electric whisk, beat together until light and fluffy. Add the flour and ground rice and, using a wooden spoon, mix together until the mixture resembles fine breadcrumbs.

2 With your hands, gather the mixture together and turn out onto a work surface. Knead gently together to form a ball.

3 Lightly roll the dough into a sausage shape, measuring about 7.5 cm/3 in thick. Wrap in baking paper and chill in the refrigerator for about 1 hour, or until firm.

4 Preheat the oven to 190°C/375°F/Gas Mark 5. Line several baking sheets with baking paper. Dust another sheet of baking paper with sugar. Unwrap the dough and roll in the sugar until evenly coated.

5 Using a sharp knife, cut the roll into rounds about 8 mm/⅜ in thick and place on the prepared baking sheets.

6 Bake in the oven for 20–25 minutes, or until set and lightly coloured. Sprinkle with sugar and leave on the baking tray for 10 minutes to cool slightly, then transfer to a wire rack and leave to cool completely.

walnut crunchies

These are cookies for walnut lovers, but other nuts, such as almonds or hazelnuts, could be used if preferred. As their title suggests, they are crisp and deep golden brown, and very moreish.

makes about 16

you will need

55 g/2 oz walnut halves

70 g/2½ oz butter or hard margarine, cut into cubes

55 g/2 oz Demerara sugar

55 g/2 oz golden syrup

1 tbsp boiling water

¾ tsp bicarbonate of soda

70 g/2½ oz plain white flour

55 g/2 oz porridge oats

1 Preheat the oven to 150°C/300°F/Gas Mark 2. Chop the walnuts into small pieces.

2 Put the butter in a large saucepan with the sugar and golden syrup. Heat gently until the butter has melted and the ingredients are runny but not hot. Stir together until combined.

3 Put the water in a cup and stir in the bicarbonate of soda. Add to the pan and stir together.

4 Add the flour, oats and chopped walnuts to the mixture and, using a wooden spoon, mix well together.

5 Place about 16 tablespoonfuls of the mixture on a baking sheet, keeping them well apart to allow room for spreading.

6 Bake the cookies in the oven for about 10 minutes, or until deep golden brown. Leave on the baking sheet for 5 minutes to cool slightly, then transfer to a wire rack and leave to cool completely. Store the cookies in a cookie jar, airtight container or tin.

butter fork cookies

These crunchy biscuits, flavoured with cinnamon, are popular in Sweden. They obviously get their name from the indentation made with the prongs of a fork – a simple task, but it gives them their attractive finish.

makes 24

you will need

115 g/4 oz butter, softened, plus extra for greasing

85 g/3 oz caster sugar

175 g/6 oz plain white flour

½ tsp ground cinnamon

1 Preheat the oven to 190°C/375°F/Gas Mark 5. Butter several large baking sheets. Put the butter and sugar in a large bowl and, using an electric whisk, beat together until light and fluffy.

2 Sift the flour and cinnamon into the bowl and mix together. With your hand, gather the mixture together.

3 Take walnut-sized pieces of the dough and roll each one into a ball between your hands. Place on the prepared baking sheets.

4 Using a fork dipped in cold water, gently press and flatten each cookie with the prongs of the fork.

5 Bake the cookies in the oven for 10–12 minutes, or until lightly coloured. Leave for 2–3 minutes on the baking sheets to cool slightly, then transfer to a wire rack and leave to cool completely. Store the cookies in a cookie jar, an airtight container or a tin.

cherry cookies

These have a lovely crumbly texture and look so attractive, each studded with an individual cherry and an almond. Enlist a child to help you, because he or she will enjoy pressing them into the dough.

makes 20

you will need

150 g/5½ oz butter or hard margarine, cut into cubes, plus extra for greasing

70 g/2½ oz caster sugar

⅛ tsp almond extract

225 g/8 oz self-raising white flour

20 glacé cherries, total weight about 100 g/3½ oz

20 whole blanched almonds, total weight about 20 g/¾ oz

1 Preheat the oven to 180°C/350°F/Gas Mark 4. Grease several large baking sheets. Put the butter in a large saucepan and heat gently until melted but not hot. Remove from the heat.

2 Add the sugar and almond extract to the pan and stir together. Add the flour and mix until a firm dough is formed.

3 Take small pieces of the dough and roll into 2.5 cm/1 in balls between your hands to make 20 cookies in total. Place on the prepared baking sheets, keeping them well apart to allow room for spreading, and flatten slightly. Gently press a cherry and an almond into the top of each cookie.

4 Bake the cookies in the oven for 10–15 minutes, or until golden brown. Leave for 2–3 minutes on the baking sheets to cool slightly, then transfer to a wire rack and leave to cool completely. Store the cookies in a cookie jar, an airtight container or a tin.

gingersnaps

Who can resist a gingersnap? Fortunately this recipe, for crisp, crunchy, sugar-coated ginger cookies, makes a large batch, and you will find that they soon disappear from the cookie jar.

makes about 36

you will need

225 g/8 oz plain white flour

1 tsp ground ginger

1 tsp bicarbonate of soda

115 g/4 oz butter or hard margarine, cut into cubes, plus extra for greasing

115 g/4 oz caster sugar, plus extra for dusting

125 ml/4 fl oz golden syrup

1 Sift together the flour, ginger and bicarbonate of soda into a large bowl.

2 Put the butter in a large saucepan with the sugar and golden syrup. Heat gently until the butter has melted and the ingredients are runny but not hot. Stir together until combined.

3 Pour the mixture into the sifted flour and mix together to form a soft dough. Put in a polythene bag and chill in the refrigerator for at least 1 hour, or until firm.

4 Preheat the oven to 180°C/350°F/Gas Mark 4. Grease several large baking sheets. Dust a sheet of baking paper with sugar. Take walnut-sized pieces of the dough and roll each one into a ball between your hands. Roll in the sugar until evenly coated, then place on the prepared baking sheets, keeping them well apart to allow room for spreading.

5 Bake the cookies in the oven for 10–15 minutes, or until golden brown. Leave for 2–3 minutes on the baking sheets to cool slightly, then transfer to a wire rack and leave to cool completely. Store the cookies in a cookie jar, an airtight container or a tin.

almond macaroons

Macaroons originated in Italy, where they are called *amaretti*. They are particularly delicious when served alone with an after-dinner coffee and are also good with creamy desserts, ice cream or fresh fruit.

makes 20

you will need

75 g/2¾ oz ground almonds

pinch of salt

125 g/4½ oz icing sugar

2 large egg whites

½ tsp almond extract

20 whole blanched almonds, total weight about 20 g/¾ oz

1. Preheat the oven to 180°C/350°F/Gas Mark 4. Line several baking sheets with rice paper. Put the ground almonds and salt in a large bowl. Sift in the icing sugar and mix well together.

2. Put the egg whites in a large bowl and whisk until soft peaks are formed and they hold their shape, but are not dry.

3. Add the almond extract and whisked egg whites to the ground almond mixture. Then, using a large metal spoon, fold in until well mixed together.

4. Put the mixture in a piping bag, fitted with a 1 cm/½ in plain nozzle, and pipe 20 rounds onto the prepared baking sheets.

5. Leave to stand for 10 minutes, or until a skin is formed, then place a blanched almond on top of each.

6. Bake the cookies in the oven for 10–12 minutes, or until golden brown and set. Leave to cool, then strip off the rice paper. Store the cookies in a cookie jar, airtight container or tin.

italian biscotti

Italian-inspired biscotti are baked twice and the result is a crisp, hard-textured cookie, which is ideal for dunking into a fine cup of coffee. This recipe gives you a choice of different fruits and nuts – use one of each.

makes 20

you will need

butter, for greasing

75 g/2¾ oz ready-to-eat dried apricots, raisins or sultanas

275 g/9½ oz plain white flour, plus extra for dusting

1 tsp baking powder

150 g/5½ oz caster sugar

75 g/2¾ oz pistachio nuts, blanched almonds or hazelnuts

2 large eggs and 1 egg yolk

1 Preheat the oven to 180°C/350°F/Gas Mark 4. Butter a large baking sheet. If using apricots, snip them into small pieces using scissors.

2 Sift the flour and baking powder into a large bowl. Stir in the sugar and your chosen fruit and nuts. Beat the eggs and egg yolk together in a small bowl, then add to the flour mixture, a little at a time, and mix together to form a soft dough.

3 Turn the dough onto a lightly floured surface and, with floured hands, knead for 2–3 minutes or until smooth. Roll into a log shape about 4 cm/1½ in thick. Place the log on the prepared baking sheet and flatten to about 2.5 cm/1 in thickness. Dust the top with flour and cut into 20 slices, but only about two-thirds of the way down through the log.

4 Bake in the oven for 20 minutes, or until slightly golden. Reduce the oven temperature to 150°C/300°F/Gas Mark 2. Leave to cool slightly then, using a serrated knife, cut into completely separate slices and put on the baking sheets. Bake the slices for 10 minutes. Turn and bake for a further 10–15 minutes, or until golden brown and crisp. Transfer to a wire rack and leave to cool. Store the biscotti in an airtight container or tin.

lemon jumbles

Jumbles, also known as 'Jambals', are an old-fashioned cookie, made with a few basic ingredients and flavoured with simple ingredients such as lemon, almond or rosewater. It is often the simplest recipes that are the best.

you will need

280 g/10 oz self-raising white flour, plus extra for dusting

140 g/5 oz butter or hard margarine, cut into cubes, plus extra for greasing

140 g/5 oz caster sugar, plus extra for dusting

finely grated rind of 1 lemon

55 g/2 oz ground almonds

1 large egg

1 Preheat the oven to 180°C/350°F/Gas Mark 4. Grease several large baking sheets. Put the flour in a large bowl. Add the butter and rub in with your fingers until the mixture resembles fine breadcrumbs. Alternatively, put the flour and butter in a food processor and, using a pulsating action, blend together to form fine breadcrumbs.

2 Stir in the sugar, lemon rind and almonds. Beat the egg in a small bowl, add to the mixture and mix together to form a smooth dough.

3 Turn the dough onto a lightly floured surface, roll into long rolls the thickness of a sausage and then cut into 10 cm/4 in lengths.

4 Shape each roll into an 'S' shape and place on the prepared baking sheets. Alternatively, the rolls can be tied into a knot or shaped into rings.

5 Bake the cookies in the oven for 15–20 minutes, or until lightly browned. Remove from the oven and dust with sugar. Transfer to a wire rack and leave to cool. Store the cookies in a cookie jar, airtight container or tin.

orangines

These orange biscuits come from France and not only complement a cup of freshly brewed coffee but are also delicious served with creamy desserts and ice cream.

makes about 30

you will need

25 g/1 oz candied orange peel

55 g/2 oz blanched almonds

55 g/2 oz butter or hard margarine, softened, plus extra for greasing

55 g/2 oz caster sugar

40 g/1½ oz plain white flour

finely grated rind 1 small orange

2 tsp fresh orange juice

1 Preheat the oven to 180°C/350°F/Gas Mark 4. Grease several large baking sheets. Put the orange peel and almonds in a food processor and blend until finely chopped.

2 Put the butter and sugar in a large bowl and, using an electric whisk, beat together until light and fluffy.

3 Add the chopped orange mixture, flour, orange rind and juice to the creamed mixture and mix well with a wooden spoon.

4 Put teaspoons of the mixture onto the prepared baking sheets, keeping them well apart to allow room for spreading.

5 Bake the cookies in the oven for 7–8 minutes, or until lightly golden brown around the edges. Leave for 2–3 minutes on the baking sheets to cool slightly, then transfer to a wire rack and leave to cool completely. Store the cookies in a cookie jar, airtight container or tin.

rocky roads

The name describes the appearance of these cookies, which are packed with nuts, dried fruit and marshmallows, and bound together with melted chocolate. They are irresistible cookies loved by both adults and children.

makes 24

you will need

150 g/5½ oz white mini marshmallows

400 g/14 oz good-quality plain chocolate, broken into pieces

100 g/3½ oz butter or hard margarine, cut into cubes

150 g/5½ oz macadamia or Brazil nuts

150 g/5½ oz glacé cherries

1 Line a 20 cm/8 in square shallow tin with baking paper, letting it hang over the edge of the tin to make it easier for lifting and removing the cookies later. Using scissors, cut the mini marshmallows in half.

2 Put the chocolate and butter into a heatproof bowl set over a saucepan of simmering water. Heat gently until the chocolate and butter have melted.

3 Remove the bowl from the heat and stir the chocolate and butter together well. Allow to cool but not set. Then add the marshmallows, nuts and cherries and stir together until the ingredients are well mixed and coated in chocolate.

4 Spread the mixture into the prepared tin, but don't press down too much because it should look like a rocky road. Leave for 3–4 hours, or until set.

5 When set, using a hot, sharp knife, cut the rocky road into 24 pieces. Store the bars in an airtight container in a cool place or in the refrigerator.

dark chocolate cookies

These are cookies for lovers of dark chocolate but it is the addition of cocoa powder, not chocolate, that makes them rich and dark. Don't omit the vanilla extract because this also brings out the chocolate flavour.

makes about 32

you will need

140 g/5 oz butter or hard margarine, softened

200 g/7 oz caster sugar

1 large egg

1 tsp vanilla extract

150 g/5½ oz plain white flour

40 g/1½ oz cocoa powder

½ tsp bicarbonate of soda

¼ tsp salt

1 Put the butter and sugar in a large bowl and, using an electric whisk, beat together until light and fluffy.

2 Beat the egg in a small bowl, add to the mixture with the vanilla extract and beat together until combined.

3 Sift the flour, cocoa powder, bicarbonate of soda and salt into the bowl, then mix together. Put the dough in a polythene bag and chill in the refrigerator for at least 1 hour, or until firm.

4 Preheat the oven to 180°C/350°F/Gas Mark 4. Line several baking sheets with baking paper. Take small pieces of the dough and roll into 2.5 cm/1 in balls between your hands. Place on the prepared baking sheets, keeping them well apart to allow room for spreading.

5 Bake the cookies in the oven for 10–15 minutes, or until set. Leave for 5 minutes on the baking sheets to cool slightly, then transfer to a wire rack and leave to cool completely. Store the cookies in an airtight container or tin.

chocolate chip cookies

There are conflicting stories about the origin of this cookie, sometimes known as The Toll House Chocolate Chip Cookie, but what we do know is that it is the favourite cookie in America.

makes about 20

you will need

115 g/4 oz butter or hard margarine, softened

75 g/2¾ oz caster sugar

75 g/2¾ oz light soft brown sugar

1 large egg

1 tsp vanilla extract

150 g/5½ oz plain white flour

½ tsp bicarbonate of soda

¼ tsp salt

150 g/5½ oz plain chocolate chips

1 Preheat the oven to 190°C/375°F/Gas Mark 5. Line several baking sheets with baking paper. Put the butter, caster sugar and brown sugar in a large bowl and, using an electric whisk, beat together until light and fluffy.

2 Beat the egg in a small bowl, add to the mixture with the vanilla extract and beat together.

3 Sift the flour, bicarbonate of soda and salt into the bowl, then mix together. Stir in the chocolate chips.

4 Drop rounded tablespoons of the mixture onto the prepared baking sheets, keeping them well apart in order to allow room for spreading.

5 Bake the cookies in the oven for 10–15 minutes, or until golden brown. Leave for 2 minutes on the baking sheets to cool slightly, then transfer to a wire rack and leave to cool completely. Store the cookies in an airtight container or tin.

chunky nut cookies

A variation on chocolate chip cookies, these cookies are packed with chocolate chunks and nuts, and the addition of porridge oats gives them a rich, oat flavour.

makes about 12

you will need

85 g/3 oz porridge oats

55 g/2 oz walnuts, pecan or macadamia nuts

85 g/3 oz butter or hard margarine, softened, plus extra for greasing

85 g/3 oz caster sugar

85 g/3 oz light soft brown sugar

1 large egg

½ tsp vanilla extract

70 g/2½ oz plain white flour

½ tsp bicarbonate of soda

175 g/6 oz plain chocolate chunks

1 Preheat the oven to 180°C/350°F/Gas Mark 4. Grease several large baking sheets. Put the oats in a food processor and blend until finely ground. Roughly chop the nuts.

2 Put the butter, caster sugar and brown sugar in a large bowl and, using an electric whisk, beat together until light and fluffy.

3 Beat the egg in a small bowl, add to the mixture with the vanilla extract and beat together.

4 Sift the flour and bicarbonate of soda into the bowl, then mix together. Stir in the ground oats, chopped nuts and the chocolate chunks.

5 Drop rounded tablespoons of the mixture onto the prepared baking sheets, keeping them at least 10 cm/4 in apart to allow room for spreading.

6 Bake the cookies in the oven for 10–15 minutes, or until golden brown around the edges. Leave for 3 minutes on the baking sheets to cool slightly, then transfer to a wire rack and leave to cool completely. Store the cookies in an airtight container or tin.

viennese fingers

These look sophisticated, but they are surprisingly easy to make even if you haven't made a batch of piped cookies before. They have a wonderful crisp yet melt-in-the-mouth texture.

makes about 16

you will need

115 g/4 oz butter or hard margarine, softened, plus extra for greasing

25 g/1 oz icing sugar

115 g/4 oz plain white flour

¼ tsp baking powder

a few drops of vanilla extract

70 g/2½ oz good-quality plain chocolate, broken into pieces

1 Preheat the oven to 180°C/350°F/Gas Mark 4. Grease several large baking sheets. Put the butter in a large bowl and, using a wooden spoon, beat until smooth. Sift in the icing sugar and beat together until light and fluffy.

2 Sift the flour and baking powder into the mixture. Add a few drops of vanilla extract and beat well together until the mixture is smooth.

3 Put the mixture in a piping bag fitted with a large star nozzle, then pipe fingers about 7.5 cm/3 in long onto the prepared baking sheets.

4 Bake the fingers in the oven for 15–20 minutes, or until lightly golden brown. Leave them for about 3 minutes on the baking sheets to cool slightly, then transfer to a wire rack and leave to cool completely.

5 When the fingers are cold, put the chocolate in a heatproof bowl set over a saucepan of simmering water, and heat gently until the chocolate has melted.

6 Dip the ends of each finger into the melted chocolate and leave to set on the wire rack. Store the cookies in an airtight container or tin.

caramel shortbread

Caramel shortbread, also known as millionaires' shortbread, perhaps because it is so rich, consists of three layers: a buttery shortbread base, a caramel filling and a chocolate topping. All are equally delicious.

makes 16

you will need

175 g/6 oz butter, softened

55 g/2 oz caster sugar

175 g/6 oz plain white flour

55 g/2 oz ground rice or semolina

for the filling

115 g/4 oz butter, cut into cubes

115 g/4 oz soft light brown sugar

2 tbsp golden syrup

400 g/14 oz can condensed milk

for the topping

200 g/7 oz good-quality plain chocolate, broken into pieces

25 g/1 oz butter

1 Preheat the oven to 160°C/325°F/Gas Mark 3. Line a 23 cm/ 9 in shallow square tin with baking paper, letting it hang over the edge of the tin. To make the base, put the butter and sugar in a large bowl and, using an electric whisk, beat until light and fluffy.

2 Add the flour and ground rice and stir together until the mixture resembles fine breadcrumbs. Turn the mixture into the prepared tin, press evenly over the base and smooth the top.

3 Bake the base in the oven for about 30 minutes, or until set and very lightly coloured. Leave to cool in the tin.

4 To make the filling, put the butter, brown sugar, golden syrup and condensed milk in a heavy-based saucepan and heat gently, stirring until melted. Bring to the boil, stirring all the time and watching that the mixture does not stick to the pan, for 7–8 minutes or until light golden brown. Pour the caramel over the base. Leave for about 2 hours, or until firm.

5 To make the topping, put the chocolate and butter into a heatproof bowl, set over a saucepan of simmering water. Heat gently until melted, stir, then pour over the caramel and spread to coat the top. When set, use a hot, sharp knife to cut into 16 squares. Store in an airtight container in a cool place.

no-cook chocolate bars

These bars, which are easy to make and require no baking, have always been a popular way to introduce children to cooking. Nevertheless, they are popular with adults too and this is a grown-up version.

you will need

115 g/4 oz digestive biscuits

200 g/7 oz good-quality plain chocolate, broken into pieces

115 g/4 oz butter or hard margarine, cut into cubes

2 tbsp golden syrup

70 g/2½ oz blanched almonds

70 g/2½ oz Brazil nuts

70 g/2½ oz hazelnuts

70 g/2½ oz glacé cherries

70 g/2½ oz sultanas

25 g/1 oz flaked almonds

1 Line an 18 cm/7 in square shallow tin with baking paper, letting it hang over the edge of the tin. Put the biscuits in a strong polythene bag and crush with a rolling pin until they are roughly broken up.

2 Put the chocolate into a heatproof bowl set over a saucepan of simmering water. Add the butter and golden syrup and heat gently, stirring occasionally, or until the chocolate and butter have melted.

3 Remove the bowl from the heat and stir well together. Add the broken biscuits, with the almonds, Brazil nuts, hazelnuts, glacé cherries and sultanas and stir together until the ingredients are well mixed and coated in chocolate.

4 Turn the mixture into the prepared tin, press down with the back of a spoon and smooth the top.

5 Sprinkle the flaked almonds over the top of the mixture and leave to cool. When cool, chill in the refrigerator for at least 2 hours, or until set.

6 When set, remove from the tin and, using a hot, sharp knife, cut into 10 bars. Store the bars in an airtight container in a cool place or in the refrigerator.

pinwheel cookies

A chocolate dough and a vanilla dough are rolled together to make these pinwheel cookies and, although the result is rather effective, they are surprisingly easy to make.

makes 18

you will need

5 7

115 g/4 oz butter or hard margarine, softened, plus extra for greasing

27.5 **55 g/2 oz caster sugar**

½ tsp vanilla extract

57 **115 g/4 oz plain white flour**

12.5 **25 g/1 oz cornflour**

2 tsp cocoa powder

milk, for brushing

1 Put the butter and sugar in a large bowl and, using an electric whisk, beat together until light and fluffy. Transfer half the mixture to a separate bowl and add the vanilla extract.

2 Sift 55 g/2 oz of the flour and 15 g/½ oz of the cornflour into the vanilla dough. Sift the remaining flour, remaining cornflour and the cocoa powder into the other half of the mixture and mix the ingredients of each bowl together with your hands to form 2 separate soft doughs.

3 On individual sheets of baking paper, roll out each piece of dough into rectangles measuring 25.5 x 18 cm/10 x 7 in. Brush the chocolate dough with a little milk and place the vanilla dough on top. Roll up the dough from the shorter edge. Wrap the roll in the baking paper and chill in the refrigerator for about 1 hour, or until firm.

4 Preheat the oven to 180°C/350°F/Gas Mark 4. Grease several large baking sheets. Cut the roll into 18 slices and place on the baking sheets. Bake for 20 minutes, or until lightly golden brown. Leave for 3 minutes on the baking sheets to cool slightly, transfer to a wire rack and leave to cool completely. Store in an airtight container or tin.

peanut butter cookies

These classic American cookies are a favourite treat for all the family, not just children. Made with butter and peanut butter, they are crunchy yet have a wonderful melt-in-the-mouth texture.

makes 30

you will need

15 g/½ oz unsalted peanuts

115 g/4 oz butter or hard margarine, softened

115 g/4 oz crunchy peanut butter

115 g/4 oz caster sugar, plus extra for dipping

115 g/4 oz light soft brown sugar

1 large egg

½ tsp vanilla extract

150 g/5½ oz plain white flour

¼ tsp baking powder

¼ tsp bicarbonate of soda

1 Preheat the oven to 190°C/375°F/Gas Mark 5. Chop the peanuts and set aside.

2 Put the butter, peanut butter, caster sugar and brown sugar in a large bowl and, using an electric whisk, beat together until combined.

3 Add the egg and vanilla extract to the mixture and whisk together. Sift the flour, baking powder and bicarbonate into the mixture and whisk to form a soft dough.

4 With floured hands, take walnut-sized pieces of the dough and roll each one into a ball between your hands. Place on several large baking sheets, keeping them well apart to allow room for spreading.

5 Dip a fork in sugar and use to flatten the cookies, making a criss-cross pattern (this will give a 'craggy' appearance when baked). Sprinkle the chopped peanuts on top of each cookie.

6 Bake the cookies in the oven for about 10 minutes, or until golden brown. Leave for 2 minutes on the baking sheets to cool slightly, then transfer to a wire rack and leave to cool completely. Store the cookies in an airtight container or tin.

refrigerator cookies

Everyone should have a batch of this cookie dough in the refrigerator. It is easy to make and, at a moment's notice, you can slice and bake a batch of cookies to order. Simply choose your favourite variation from the recipe.

makes about 28

you will need

225 g/8 oz plain white flour, plus extra for dusting

1 tsp baking powder

115 g/4 oz butter or hard margarine, plus extra for greasing

175 g/6 oz caster sugar

55 g/2 oz flavouring of your choice, such as desiccated coconut, finely chopped sultanas, walnuts, glacé cherries or grated plain chocolate

1 large egg

1 tsp vanilla extract

1 Put the flour, baking powder and butter in a food processor and, using a pulsating action, blend together to form fine breadcrumbs. Add the sugar and the flavouring of your choice to the mixture and stir together. Beat the egg in a small bowl, add to the mixture with the vanilla extract and mix together to form a soft dough.

2 On a lightly floured surface, shape the dough into a log about 5 cm/2 in in diameter. Wrap the log in greaseproof paper and then foil and chill in the refrigerator for at least 8 hours. Alternatively, store in the freezer, then slice and bake from frozen.

3 When ready to bake, preheat the oven to 190°C/375°F/Gas Mark 5. Grease a baking sheet. Slice the dough into cookies measuring 1 cm/½ in thick and place on the prepared baking sheet, keeping them well apart to allow room for spreading. Return the remaining dough to the refrigerator and store for up to 1 week, or in the freezer for longer.

4 Bake the cookies in the oven for about 10 minutes, or until golden brown. Leave for 2 minutes on the baking sheet to cool slightly, then transfer to a wire rack and leave to cool completely. Store the cookies in an airtight container or tin.

apricot flapjacks

Flapjacks are a favourite old-fashioned bar cookie but, with the addition of apricots and cranberries, they are extra special. These flapjacks, because they contain flour, are soft and chewy like the shop-bought varieties.

makes 12

you will need

115 g/4 oz ready-to-eat dried apricots

225 g/8 oz butter or hard margarine, cut into cubes, plus extra for greasing

175 g/6 oz caster sugar

4 tbsp golden syrup

55 g/2 oz dried cranberries

280 g/10 oz jumbo porridge oats

115 g/4 oz self-raising white flour

1 Preheat the oven to 180°C/350°F/Gas Mark 4. Grease a 23 cm/9 in square shallow tin. Chop the apricots into small pieces and set aside.

2 Put the butter into a large saucepan with the sugar and golden syrup. Heat gently until the butter has melted and the ingredients are runny but not hot. Stir together until combined.

3 Remove the saucepan from the heat, add the chopped apricots with the cranberries, oats and flour and stir until well mixed together.

4 Turn the mixture into the prepared tin, press down with the back of a spoon and smooth the top.

5 Bake the flapjack mixture in the oven for about 25 minutes, or until golden brown. Cut into bars whilst still hot, then leave to cool in the tin before serving.

snowflake cookies

Make a batch of these before Christmas to give as a gift, to hang on the Christmas tree – or simply to eat, if the temptation is too much. The only problem you might have is making them last until Christmas Day.

you will need

200 g/7 oz self-raising white flour, plus extra for dusting

1 tsp ground mixed spice

100 g/3½ oz butter or hard margarine

1 large egg

100 g/3½ oz light soft brown sugar

for the icing

225 g/8 oz icing sugar

3–4 tsp water

silver or gold dragées (cake decorating balls), to decorate

1 Preheat the oven to 180°C/350°F/Gas Mark 4. Line several large baking sheets with baking paper. Put the flour, mixed spice and butter in a food processor and, using a pulsating action, blend together to form fine breadcrumbs.

2 Beat the egg in a small bowl, add to the mixture with the brown sugar and mix together to form a smooth dough.

3 Turn the dough onto a lightly floured surface and roll out thinly to a thickness of about 5 mm/¼ in. Using a 6.5 cm/2½ in star cutter, cut out stars and place on the prepared baking sheets. If you wish to hang the cookies on the Christmas tree, make a hole in a point of each cookie with a large skewer.

4 Bake in the oven for 10–15 minutes, or until golden brown. Push a skewer in the holes again so that they remain open. Leave for 2 minutes on the baking sheets to cool slightly, then transfer to a wire rack and leave to cool completely.

5 When the cookies are cold, make the icing. Sift the icing sugar into a large bowl and add enough water to make a thick, smooth icing. Using a teaspoon, drop the icing onto the cookies and smooth over, then decorate with silver or gold dragées. Leave to set. To hang the cookies, thread narrow ribbon through the hole of each.

jumbo sultana cookies

It is probably the large size of these cookies that children find so appealing but, packed with sultanas, oats and desiccated coconut, they are also healthy and taste great too.

you will need

115 g/4 oz butter or hard margarine, softened, plus extra for greasing

115 g/4 oz caster sugar

115 g/4 oz light soft brown sugar

2 large eggs

½ tsp vanilla extract

175 g/6 oz plain white flour

½ tsp baking powder

¼ tsp bicarbonate of soda

85 g/3 oz porridge oats

100 g/3½ oz sultanas

50 g/1¾ oz desiccated coconut

1 Preheat the oven to 190°C/375°F/Gas Mark 5. Grease several large baking sheets. Put the butter, caster sugar and brown sugar in a large bowl and, using an electric whisk, beat together until light and fluffy.

2 Beat the eggs in a small bowl, add to the mixture with the vanilla extract and mix together until combined.

3 Sift the flour, baking powder and bicarbonate of soda into the bowl. Add the oats, sultanas and coconut and then mix together well.

4 Place large rounded tablespoons of the mixture onto the prepared baking sheets, keeping them well apart to allow room for spreading, and flatten slightly with the back of a wooden spoon.

5 Bake the cookies in the oven for about 15 minutes, or until golden brown. Leave for 2 minutes on the baking sheet to cool slightly, then transfer to a wire rack and leave to cool completely. Store the cookies in an airtight container or tin.

gingerbread boys

Children need no encouragement to make these character cookies, and it would be wise to have a plentiful supply of sweets, because many will get eaten before they are used to decorate them.

makes about 14

you will need

350 g/12 oz plain white flour, plus extra for dusting

1 tsp bicarbonate of soda

1 tsp ground ginger

1 tsp ground cinnamon

115 g/4 oz butter or hard margarine, plus extra for greasing

1 large egg

175 g/6 oz light soft brown sugar

100 ml/3½ fl oz golden syrup

to decorate

various coloured tubes of writing icing

plentiful supply of colourful chocolate sugar-coated sweets

1 Preheat the oven to 190°C/375°F/Gas Mark 5. Grease several large baking sheets. Put the flour, bicarbonate of soda, ginger, cinnamon and butter in a food processor and, using a pulsating action, blend together to form fine breadcrumbs.

2 Beat the egg in a small bowl, add to the mixture with the sugar and golden syrup and mix together to form a smooth dough.

3 Turn the dough onto a lightly floured surface and roll out thinly to a thickness of about 5 mm/¼ in. Using a gingerbread-man cutter, cut out figures and place on the prepared baking sheets. Continue until all the dough has been used.

4 Using a garlic press, push some of the dough through it to make strings of hair and arrange on the heads of the figures.

5 Bake the cookies in the oven for 10–15 minutes, or until the edges are firm. Leave for 2 minutes on the baking sheet to cool slightly, then transfer to a wire rack and leave to cool completely.

6 When cold, use the writing icing to create the eyes and mouth, and to stick sweets down their fronts to resemble buttons. Store the cookies in an airtight container or tin.

iced cookie cutouts

In America, it is popular to make these at Christmas time, when children enjoy icing and decorating them. For grown-up versions, they are very good left plain, served with coffee and eaten at any time of the year.

makes about 55

you will need

150 g/5½ oz butter or hard margarine, softened

150 g/5½ oz caster sugar

1 small egg

¾ tsp vanilla extract

¾ tsp almond extract

250 g/9 oz plain white flour, plus extra for dusting

pinch of salt

for the icing

500 g/1 lb 2 oz icing sugar

8–9 tsp water

edible food colourings (optional)

to decorate

cake decorating sprinkles (optional)

various coloured tubes of writing icing (optional)

1 Preheat the oven to 190°C/375°F/Gas Mark 5. Line several large baking sheets with baking paper. Put the butter and sugar in a large bowl and, using an electric whisk, beat together until light and fluffy. Beat the egg in a small bowl, add to the mixture with the vanilla extract and almond extract and beat together. Sift the flour and salt into the bowl, then beat together.

2 Turn the dough onto a lightly floured surface and roll out thinly to a thickness of about 3 mm/⅛ in. Using a selection of 6–7.5 cm/ 2½–3 in cookie cutters, cut out shapes and place on the prepared baking sheets. Continue until all the dough has been used.

3 Bake in the oven for 6–8 minutes, or until lightly golden brown. Leave for 2 minutes on the baking sheet to cool slightly, then transfer to a wire rack and leave to cool completely.

4 When the cookies are cold, make the icing. Sift the icing sugar into a large bowl and add enough water to make a thick, smooth icing. If using, dip a skewer into the food colouring, then stir into the icing. Make additional bowls for additional colours. Using a teaspoon, drop the icing onto the cookies and smooth over, then decorate to your taste. Leave to set.

coconut macaroons

Crisp on the outside and soft in the centre, these old-fashioned home-made cookies are light and fluffy – unlike the commercial variety, which tend to be dense and sweet. They are loved by children and coconut lovers alike.

you will need

6 glacé cherries, total weight about 25 g/1 oz

150 g/5½ oz desiccated coconut

50 g/1¾ oz ground almonds

2 large egg whites

115 g/4 oz caster sugar

1   Preheat the oven to 180°C/350°F/Gas Mark 4. Line several large baking sheets with rice paper or baking paper. Cut the cherries in half.

2   Put the desiccated coconut and ground almonds in a bowl and mix together.

3   Put the egg whites in a large bowl and whisk until soft peaks are formed and they hold their shape, but are not dry.

4   Add the sugar to the egg whites and, using a large metal spoon, fold in until incorporated. Add the coconut mixture and fold in until well mixed together.

5   Drop 12 large rounded tablespoons of the mixture in domes onto the prepared baking sheets. Place a glacé cherry half on top of each dome of mixture to decorate.

6   Bake the cookies in the oven for about 15 minutes, or until lightly golden brown around the edges. Leave to cool, then strip off the rice paper. Store the cookies in an airtight container or tin.

decorating ideas

When cookies are prepared for Christmas, special occasions and for children, this is the time to be creative and decorate your cookies. You could even hold a children's cookie decorating party.

You need to start with a batch of cookies that have been cut into shapes with a cookie cutter, such as gingerbread men, animal shapes, Christmas-themed cutters and stars. Stars are particularly versatile because they can be used for Christmas and other special occasions or written on with a message of congratulations. A round, fluted cutter is also adaptable because it can be used as a base for children to write their name on, or to decorate as a flower, smiley face, spiderweb or other decorative motif.

To make glacé icing, you will need 115 g/4 oz icing sugar and 2–3 teaspoons of water. This is sufficient to coat about 24 cookies. The icing should be moist enough to ensure that the coating is smooth – but not so moist that it runs off the cookies. If wished, the icing can be coloured with edible food colourings. Add the colouring by dipping a skewer into the bottle and adding a few drops at a time. Apply the icing quickly and add any decoration before the icing sets.

Once the icing has dried, additional icing can be piped on top. This can be home-made, piped with a small writing nozzle, or you can buy various coloured tubes of ready-made writing icing.

Decorations could include sprinkles, silver and gold balls (dragées), crystallised flowers and various chocolate decorations.

Almost any variety of cookie can be decorated with chocolate, simply by dipping it in melted chocolate, or piping or drizzling chocolate on top. Use a good-quality plain chocolate to add a sophisticated touch.

Finally, when it comes to serving or giving, the presentation of cookies can make all the difference, so seek out pretty gift boxes and tins and line with greaseproof paper, or pack into clear cellophane and then tie with ribbon for a pretty finishing touch.

index

acknowledgements

Bright Ideas,
38 High Street,
Lewes,
East Sussex
BN7 2LU

Steamer Trading,
20/21 High Street,
Lewes,
East Sussex
BN7 2BY